Library of Congress Cataloging-in-Publication Data

Winter, Jonah.
The fabulous feud of Gilbert & Sullivan / by Jonah Winter ;
illustrated by Richard Egielski. — 1st ed.   p. cm.
Summary: In the late nineteenth century, Mr. Gilbert and Mr. Sullivan, who write operas together
for a theater called Topsy-Turvydom, have a falling-out when Mr. Sullivan refuses to write music
for another ridiculous story that is like all the others.
ISBN 978-0-439-93050-5 (hardcover) 1. Gilbert, W. S. (William Schwenck), 1836-1911—Juvenile fiction.
2. Sullivan, Arthur, Sir, 1842-1900—Juvenile fiction. [1. Gilbert, W. S. (William Schwenck), 1836-1911—Fiction. 2. Sullivan, Arthur,
Sir, 1842-1900—Fiction. 3. Composers—Fiction. 4. Authors—Fiction. 5. Operetta—Fiction.
6. Great Britain—History—Victoria, 1837-1901—Fiction.] I. Egielski, Richard, ill. II. Title. III.
Title: Fabulous feud of Gilbert and Sullivan.
PZ7.W75477Fab 2009   [E]—dc22   2008027027
ISBN-13: 978-0-439-93050-5 · ISBN-10: 0-439-93050-2
10 9 8 7 6 5 4 3 2 1   09 10 11 12 13

The art for this book was created using Pitt India ink pens and Holbein watercolors on Arches 300 lb.,
hot press watercolor paper. Book design by Elizabeth B. Parisi

First edition, April 2009
Printed in Singapore 46

To Sally, with love
and gratitude
—JW

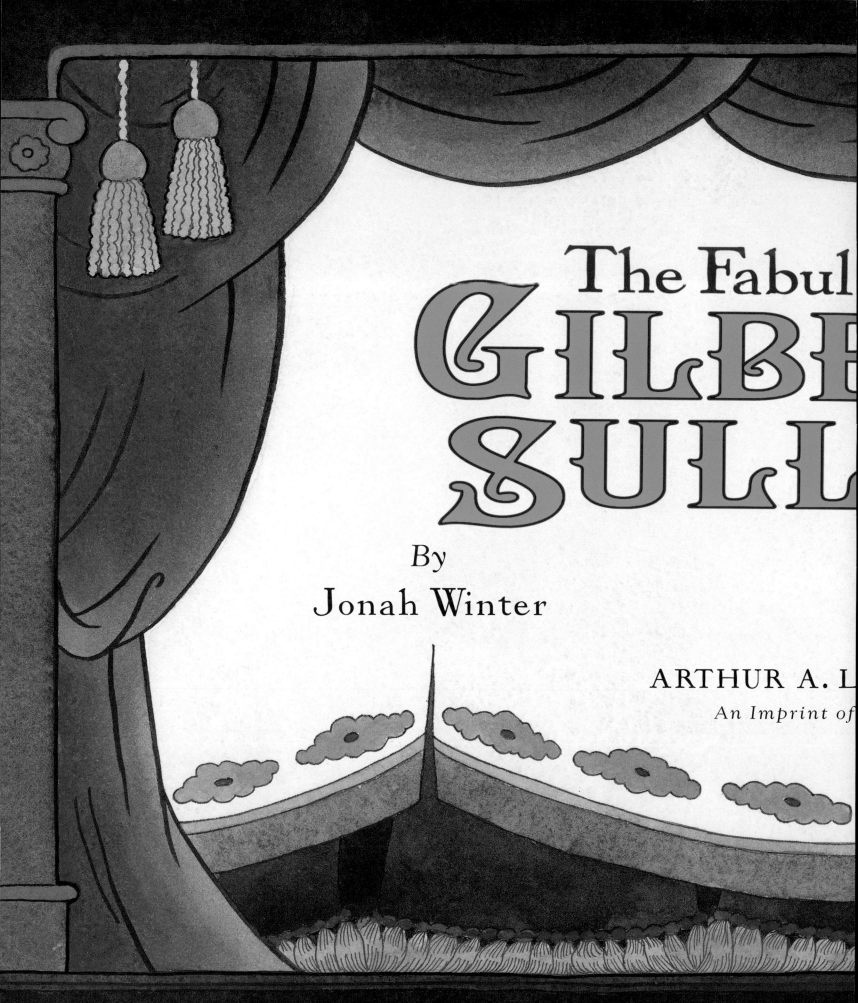

The Fabul...
GILBE...
SULL...

By

Jonah Winter

ARTHUR A. L...

An Imprint of

ous Feud of

ERT &

IVAN

Illustrated By

Richard Egielski

EVINE BOOKS

Scholastic Inc.

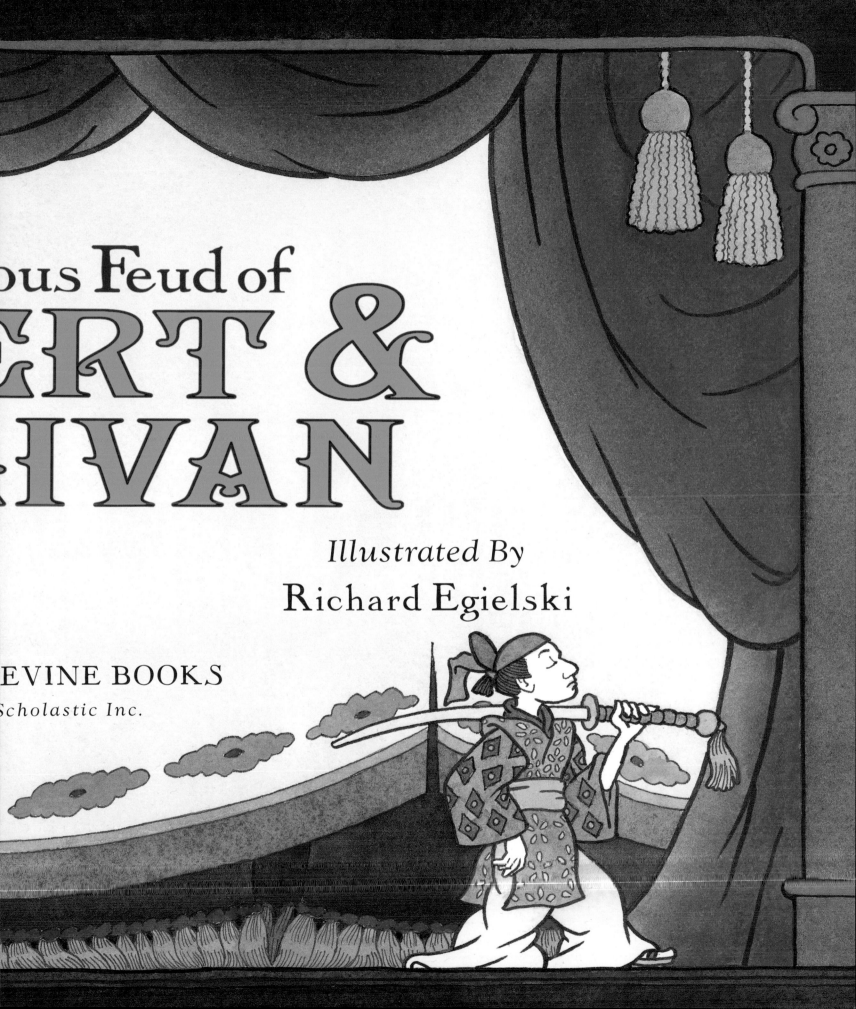

There was a time when jolly old
England was not so jolly.
Children worked in factories.
Queen Victoria frowned.
Everything was grim.
Everything was dark — except . . . in the
make-believe kingdom of Topsy-Turvydom.

Topsy-Turvydom wasn't really a kingdom. It was an opera stage where grown-ups acted silly, and everything got very, very, very confused.

Fairies with battery-operated wings got married to stuffy old men in bad wigs.

Pirates and policemen sang rousing songs together.

Fake ghosts with false mustaches got into polite arguments with living persons. Such was the kingdom of Topsy-Turvydom.

And in this kingdom, there were two kings. Well, they weren't really *kings*. They were two gentlemen: Mr. Gilbert . . . and Mr. Sullivan. You see, they were the ones who wrote these operas.

Mr. Gilbert wrote the words. In a big, dark room filled with things from all over the world, he dreamt up ridiculous stories for the operas. Actually, it was more or less the *same* ridiculous story for *every* opera — but set in different places . . .

on a boat,

in Italy,

in a castle, and yet . . .

always the same story!

This drove Mr. Sullivan crazy. He wrote the music for these operas.
And he longed, more than anything, to write a *serious* opera, a *grand* opera.
In his moonlit parlor, he sat at the piano playing beautiful melodies,
dreaming of a grand romantic opera. . . .

And then the telephone rang.

It was Mr. Gilbert.

"Mr. Sullivan?" said Mr. Gilbert.

"Mr. Gilbert," said Mr. Sullivan. "Well, what is it?"

"I have a new opera —"

"NO," said Mr. Sullivan, and he slammed down the phone.

Mr. Gilbert was stunned. What sort of way was that for a man to treat his friend? Mr. Sullivan had never acted this way before. Had Mr. Gilbert done something wrong? What about his new opera? *Dear, dear, dear,* sighed Mr. Gilbert. *This is very tiresome.*

And he sat up half the night trying to figure out why his old friend had hung up on him.

The next day the sun was shining brightly, but the problem still remained: Mr. Sullivan had behaved very rudely and strangely. It was a mystery to Mr. Gilbert, and he intended to solve it. So he called Mr. D'Oyly Carte, the man who owned the Savoy Theater. A meeting was arranged.

And this meeting did not go well at all.

"I refuse to write any more music for Mr. Gilbert's *ridiculous* operas," said Mr. Sullivan. "It's always the same *ridiculous* story, over and over and over again!"

"I beg your pardon," cried Mr. Gilbert. "My operas are NOT *ridiculous!*"

"Yes, they are!"

"No, they're aren't!"

"Yes, they are!"

"NO. THEY. AREN'T!!!" cried Mr. Gilbert, and with THAT, he left the meeting in a huff. *The nerve of Mr. Sullivan,* he thought. *Well, if that's all the thanks I'm going to get from Mr. Sullivan, then FINE. He can just ROT, as far as I'm concerned....*

And so it was, that the two kings of Topsy-Turvydom parted ways. Mr. Sullivan took a vacation — to France! He ate wonderful food, went to concerts, and did his best to forget about his argument with Mr. Gilbert.

Meanwhile, Mr. Gilbert huffed and puffed and grumbled and mumbled, still angry at how he had been treated. He didn't feel like writing. He didn't feel like doing anything. He never wanted to see Mr. Sullivan again.

Well, here was a fine howdy-do! Here was a pretty mess! Here was a state of things! When Mr. Sullivan returned from his trip, he felt exactly the same: No more silly operas, thank you very much!

And yet, in the kingdom of Topsy-Turvydom, things have a way of getting turned on their heads. Mr. Gilbert missed his old friend. And as time passed, he knew that if they were to write more operas together, he would have to come up with something *completely* different....

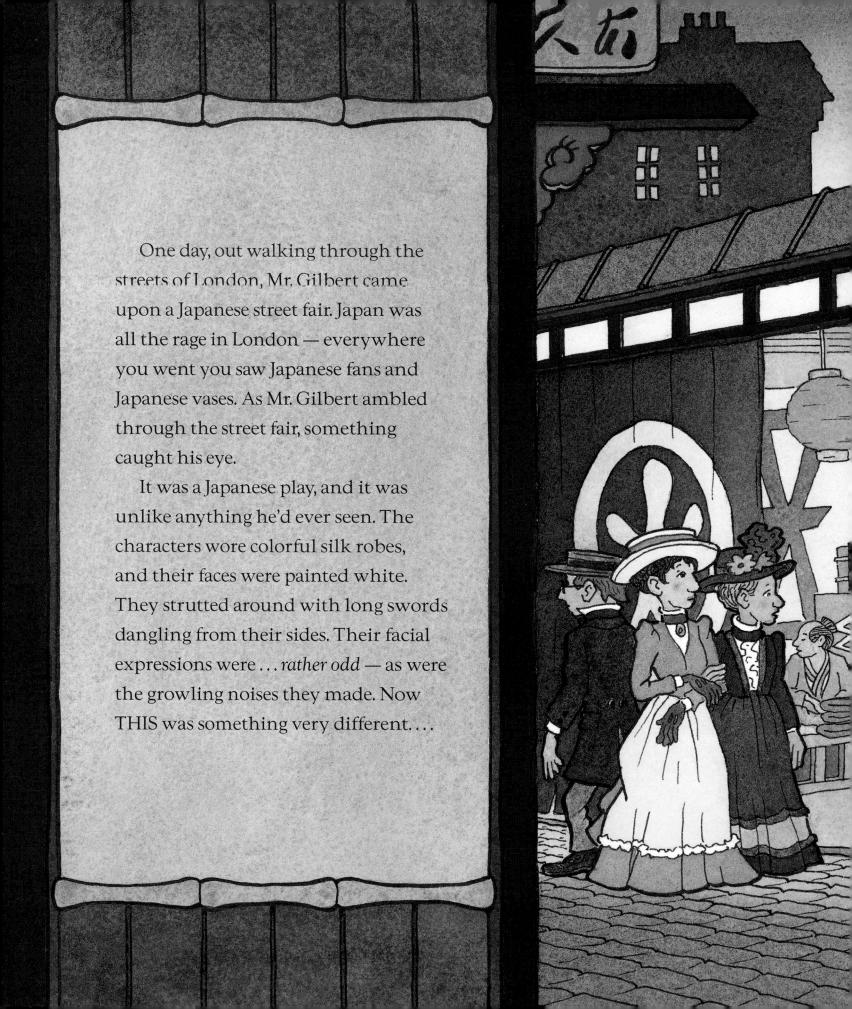

One day, out walking through the streets of London, Mr. Gilbert came upon a Japanese street fair. Japan was all the rage in London — everywhere you went you saw Japanese fans and Japanese vases. As Mr. Gilbert ambled through the street fair, something caught his eye.

It was a Japanese play, and it was unlike anything he'd ever seen. The characters wore colorful silk robes, and their faces were painted white. They strutted around with long swords dangling from their sides. Their facial expressions were … *rather odd* — as were the growling noises they made. Now THIS was something very different. . . .

Back home, he sat down at his desk with a blank piece of paper. He sat and he sat, trying to think of something Mr. Sullivan would like — an opera that would be *nothing* like anything he'd ever written. As he daydreamed, his eyes gazed lazily across the room — then fixed on a single point:

A Japanese sword hung upon the wall. "Aha!" Mr. Gilbert exclaimed. He took down the sword and held it in his hands. It was quite heavy, and he could barely hold it. *And just like that, he knew what his next opera would be about!*

He set to work at once, writing and writing for days and days. When he had finished the story, he hurried to Mr. Sullivan's house, with his manuscript under his arm. It was raining, but Mr. Gilbert didn't care. He couldn't wait to see Mr. Sullivan!

Mr. Sullivan heard the knock at the door, and he peered out the window at his old friend. Seeing him standing out there in the rain, Mr. Sullivan felt sad. Tears filled his eyes. He rushed to the door.

"My good sir," said Mr. Gilbert, with a faint smile. "I have something *I think you're going to like.*"

Without even removing his hat, he began reading Mr. Sullivan his new opera story. It was set in Japan, of course. And it was called . . . *The Mikado* or . . . *The Town of Titipu.*

"I don't think I quite caught that last remark," said Mr. Sullivan, choking back a laugh. "Did you say . . . Titipu . . . ?!"

"You are quite correct, sir," said Mr. Gilbert. "Titipu."

"Titipu?"

"Titipu."

The story continued. It was about a cowardly executioner named Ko-Ko.

" . . . and then Ko-Ko tricks Nanki-Poo into marrying Yum-Yum . . ."

"I see," said Mr. Sullivan when Mr. Gilbert had finished. He was beaming. "Nothing could *possibly* be more satisfactory!"

This *was* a very silly story, and yet . . . Mr. Sullivan loved it! It was new. It was different. There was not a single magic potion in the whole story — this was progress! He set to work on the music right away — and just like that, Mr. Gilbert and Mr. Sullivan were partners once again.

As Mr. Sullivan wrote the music, Mr. Gilbert went back home and played with a model theater and little wooden actors and actresses. This is how he figured out how the opera would look, and how the characters would move.

It may have looked silly — but it worked. Somehow, these little wooden figures turned into live human beings. And when the curtain rose on opening night, it was a stunning sight: A stage full of Englishmen dressed up to look Japanese, with white face paint, black wigs, and swords dangling from their sides.

It was ridiculous — and beautiful! It was *completely different!*

It was the best music Mr. Sullivan had ever written — and the funniest words Mr. Gilbert had ever written. The audience applauded as they never had before, and the two kings of Topsy-Turvydom took their bows, side by side. Could they have gotten here without the arguing? Who knows? Sometimes even the best of friends fight. One thing is for certain, though: Had they not made up, their greatest opera would never have been written. They needed each other.

After *The Mikado*, Mr. Gilbert and Mr. Sullivan
went on to write five more operas together. *And they still
fought from time to time. . . .*

Author's Note

GILBERT & SULLIVAN, though their names are usually mentioned together, were, in fact, two separate people.

William Schwenck Gilbert was born in London, England, on November 18, 1836, and he died on May 29, 1911. Arthur Seymour Sullivan was born in Lambeth, England, on May 13, 1842, and he died on November 22, 1900. For two men who created so many beautiful operas together, they were quite different in their personalities and artistic goals.

W. S. Gilbert, who wrote the words for their operas, was a gruff, argumentative man whose wittiness was hard to match. He had no delusions of grandeur artistically, but sought primarily to entertain his audiences with puns, jokes, funny rhymes, and fundamentally ridiculous plot-lines often referred to as "topsy-turvy" by critics. Though he wrote plays and words for songs before and after his collaboration with Arthur Sullivan, those are generally regarded as weak compared with the highly original work he created with Mr. Sullivan.

Sir Arthur Sullivan, on the other hand, was a more mild-mannered gentleman who, unlike Mr. Gilbert, most definitely had delusions of grandeur (and, as the "Sir" suggests, he was indeed knighted!). His dream was to write a serious, grand opera, and he was quite bitter at having instead to write the music for Mr. Gilbert's very silly words. Like Mr. Gilbert, though, Mr. Sullivan was largely un-successful in his attempts to go it alone. The music he composed before and after his collaboration with Gilbert is largely ignored.

Together, though, these two odd bedfellows created fourteen very special operas: *Thespis, Trial by Jury, The Sorcerer, H.M.S. Pinafore, The Pirates of Penzance, Patience, Iolanthe, Princess Ida, The Mikado, Ruddigore, The Yeomen of the Guard, The Gondoliers, Utopia Limited*, and *The Grand Duke*. Though very Victorian, and very English, these operas continue to enjoy unrivaled popularity throughout the world, especially in America. As a body of dramatic works, they are perform-ed more often than any other plays or operas in the English language — including Shakespeare! This is because of the universal appeal of their wit, gorgeous music, and genuine human themes (regardless of the silly plotlines).

Gilbert & Sullivan took the Italian opera form and turned it into something new — something English, down-to-earth, and not quite so grand or long or serious. What they created in this new opera form provided the basis for the modern musical comedies of Broadway in America. Without Gilbert & Sullivan, who knows if the modern musical would have been invented?

For more information on Gilbert & Sullivan, and to hear a few clips, the following Web site is quite helpful: http://math.boisestate.edu/GaS/. And, you never know, you might even find that there is a Gilbert & Sullivan society near you!